AF143836

BOOK ANALYSIS

By Kody Coughlan

The Last Tycoon

BY F. SCOTT FITZGERALD

F. SCOTT FITZGERALD

AMERICAN FICTION WRITER

- **Born in Minnesota, United States in 1896.**
- **Died in California, United States in 1940.**
- **Notable works:**
  - *This Side of Paradise* (1920), novel
  - *Tales of the Jazz Age* (1920), short story collection
  - *The Great Gatsby* (1925), novel

Francis Scott Fitzgerald was a fiction writer whose novels depicting the Jazz Age (an era in the 1920s in which jazz music and dance developed and emerged) are greatly celebrated to this day. Fitzgerald was born to Edward – an aristocrat – and Mary ("Mollie") McQuillan Fitzgerald.

Fitzgerald attended St. Paul Academy in Minnesota from 1908 to 1910, and Newman School in New Jersey from 1911 to 1913. It was not until he attended Princeton that he realised his potential, and his dream of becoming successful. Fitzgerald became a key figure in the university's literary cohort, and was later elected into one of the top societies at Princeton.

After flunking out of Princeton, and attempting to rejoin, Fitzgerald joined the army in 1917. During his time there, he met Zelda Sayre (American socialite and writer, 1900-1948), with whom he fell in love and later married in 1920.

THE LAST TYCOON

POSTHUMOUS UNFINISHED NOVEL

- **Genre:** unfinished novel
- **Reference edition:** Fitzgerald, F. S. (1941) *The Last Tycoon*. United States: Charles Scribner's Sons.
- **1st edition:** 1941
- **Themes:** death, jealousy, the American Dream, social class, relationships

Published posthumously, *The Last Tycoon* draws on Fitzgerald's own experiences as a screenwriter within its pages. It follows the life of Monroe Stahr, a Hollywood studio manager who is based on the then-head of Metro-Goldwyn-Mayer, Irving Thalberg (1899-1936), through his rise and fall from power in Hollywood. The story is told through a mix of first-person and third-person narrations, with the main narrator being Cecelia Brady. *The Last Tycoon* was unfinished at the time of Fitzgerald's death, and his close friend Edmund Wilson (American writer and critic, 1895-1972) put the book together from Fitzgerald's own notes, along with six already completed chapters and a short conclusion.

SUMMARY

THE TRAVEL TO LOS ANGELES

The novel opens with the main narrator, Cecilia Brady, who is the daughter of the Hollywood producer Pat Brady, flying home after spending time away at college in New York. While on the plane, Cecilia meets an old family friend, Wylie Whyte, a screenwriter, along with his companion, Mr. Schwartz. Mr. Schwartz, though it is not explained to Cecilia right away, is a producer with an unsuccessful career.

The plane is forced to land in Nashville, Tennessee due to complications during the flight. Upon landing, the three – Cecilia, Wylie, and Mr. Schwartz – head to Hermitage, the famous home of Andrew Jackson (American president, 1767-1845). During the long ride to the house, Mr. Schwartz falls asleep, leaving Wylie flirting with Cecilia.

Unfortunately, when they arrive at Hermitage, it is not yet open as it is only dawn. Instead, Wylie and Cecilia talk on the steps of the house as Mr.

Schwartz sleeps on. As he wakes and the group gets ready to depart, however, Mr. Schwartz informs Wylie and Cecilia that he has decided not to continue his journey to Los Angeles. He gives a note to Wylie, asking him to give it to a fellow traveller, and Wylie and Cecilia leave him behind in Nashville. Soon after, Mr. Schwartz commits suicide, and Wylie and Cecilia do not find out until one day later.

The note, it is soon found out, is for Cecilia's business partner, Monroe Stahr. Cecilia admits that she has had a crush on Stahr for a long time, and perhaps this summer will provide the opportunity that they need to explore those feelings even more.

MONROE STAHR AND THE WOMAN OF THE FLOOD

While at her father's studio, an earthquake traps Cecilia, her father, and his business partners in Stahr's office. The back lot of the studio is flooded due to a water main bursting. The group go outside to see the damage done for themselves. Two women are seen floating along on a prop, and Stahr is immediately stunned by one of the women's uncanny resemblance to his deceased wife.

The next day, Stahr persuades his secretary to find and identify the girls. After a while, their efforts bear fruit when one of the girls is found and agrees to meet Stahr, though reluctantly. As soon as he sees her, however, he realises that this is the wrong girl, as she looks nothing like his wife. Nevertheless, she requests that he meet a friend of hers. Instantly, Stahr recognises the second girl to be the one he is looking for.

When she refuses his offer to meet him or to even tell him her name, however, he leaves feeling disheartened. Later, he meets the same girl at a party, and manages to convince her to get coffee with him. He discovers her name – Kathleen – and the two travel to Santa Monica, where Stahr shows her a house that he is currently building. Kathleen seems quite uncertain and hesitant to be with Stahr, though her further insistence that they return to the house tells him a different story. After returning, the two become intimate. However, Stahr later learns that Kathleen is engaged to another man.

Despite Stahr trying to convince Kathleen not to marry this other man, his advances do not work. Kathleen sends him a telegram informing him that she is now married.

CECILIA AND STAHR

Stahr approaches Cecilia about accompanying him to a meeting with a presumed communist who wishes to organise a labour union within the film studio. The two meet the man over dinner, where Stahr drinks excessively. He gets into a physical confrontation with the communist, and after Cecilia attends to his wounds, she and Stahr grow close and start to date.

Cecilia's father, Mr. Brady, takes a poor view of Cecilia and Stahr's relationship. Brady starts plotting to drive Stahr out of the company, going as far as to use Stahr's affair with Kathleen, which has continued in spite of her marriage, as blackmail. Brady then hires a man to murder Stahr, and in retaliation, Stahr does the same. Nevertheless, Stahr begins to rethink his choice, but he never has the chance to prevent the assassination, as he is killed in a plane crash. Soon after, Brady also dies, and Cecilia is left heartbroken, having lost the two men who meant the most to her.

CHARACTER STUDY

MONROE STAHR

Monroe Stahr is a 35-year-old film producer based in Los Angeles. He is the business partner of Pat Brady, the father of Cecilia. Unlike Brady, who is solely interested in profits, Stahr is also interested in the artistic value of films: he is keen on creating and using his artistic ability to tell stories instead of just making money, although he does not disregard profit entirely.

Stahr's wife has recently passed away, and Stahr has buried himself in his work ever since as a coping mechanism to distract him from his grief. Despite the inherently social nature of his career as a businessman and producer, Stahr also isolates himself from others and generally works alone, ostensibly to boost his productivity. This means that he tends to focus obsessively on his work, to the detriment of all else. Nonetheless, Stahr is loyal to his beliefs.

By the start of the novel, the long years of obsessing over his work have taken their toll, and Stahr is almost completely burned out. He is also said to be battling with schizophrenia – a fight which he is losing.

During the novel, Stahr falls in love with a woman, Kathleen, because of how much she reminds him of his late wife. Despite her initial refusal to see Stahr, Kathleen eventually agrees to meet him. After an intimate evening with Kathleen, Stahr discovers that she is engaged, and begins trying to convince her to call off the engagement. He later finds out that his efforts were in vain, as Kathleen has married her fiancé.

Like Fitzgerald's previous novel *The Great Gatsby* (1925), each character in the novel is based on an individual he knew in real life. Stahr is modelled after Metro-Goldwyn-Mayer's Irving Thalberg, and is portrayed as a confident and authoritative leader who uses skill and force to exercise that authority in the workplace.

CECILIA BRADY

Cecilia is the narrator of the majority of the story. She is the daughter of the Hollywood producer Pat Brady and is in love with Monroe Stahr.

Throughout the novel, she unsuccessfully tries to win his heart in return.

At the beginning of the novel, Cecilia is travelling home from college in order to visit her father in Los Angeles. It is during her travels that she meets Wylie White, a young screenwriter who flirts with Cecilia to gain her, and thus, her father's, trust. As her father is a producer, and Whyte works within the industry, he wishes to get close to Cecilia's father in order to have contacts in the film industry.

Being the daughter of a producer, Cecilia has a clear insight into both the inner workings and the pitfalls of the film industry. When her father no longer wants Stahr around, Cecilia informs him of Stahr's relationship with Kathleen, which is used as blackmail. In the end, both of the men Cecilia loves – her father and Stahr – end up dead, and she is left alone when the story finishes.

PAT BRADY

Pat Brady is the business partner of Monroe Stahr. In contrast to Stahr, who values the artistic quality of films, Brady is only interested in making money. His personality is the polar opposite of Stahr's, as is his understanding of the industry they work in. Brady is cold and manipulative, and understands very little about the technical side of the film industry.

While Stahr is modelled after Irving Thalberg, Brady is modelled after Louis B. Mayer (1884-1957), another top executive at Metro-Goldwyn-Mayer. During his time at the company, Mayer mainly liaised with MGM's corporate headquarters, while also being responsible for hiring and firing employees. In contrast, Thalberg had closer contact with the production units and employees.

It is Brady's goal throughout the novel to get rid of Stahr. In order to do this, Brady hires a man to kill Stahr for him. Unbeknownst to Brady, his actions are echoed by Stahr, who hires another hitman to kill Brady. Brady's plan fails, due to Stahr being killed in a plane crash. However, Brady is killed by Stahr's hitman, leaving both men dead by the end of the novel.

ANALYSIS

INSPIRATIONS BEHIND *THE LAST TYCOON*

The Last Tycoon follows characters within the film industry, including producers and screenwriters, amongst many others. The inspiration for this novel came from Fitzgerald's own experiences within this industry, where he worked as a screenwriter from 1937 right up until his death in 1940.

> "Sadly, most of his work was to no avail. Billy Wilder, Fitzgerald's friend and admirer in his Hollywood days, always thought the notion of turning him into a screenwriter was a little misguided. He once compared Fitzgerald to 'a great sculptor who is hired to do a plumbing job'." (McGrath, 2004)

However, between 1927 and 1931, Fitzgerald worked for Irving Thalberg, the head of MGM and the individual he modelled Monroe Stahr after. Before MGM, Thalberg worked at Universal Pictures, first as an office secretary, and then as a personal secretary to the president of Universal, Carl Laemmle (American film producer, 1867-1939).

Despite being young and inexperienced in the world of filmmaking, Thalberg managed to impress Laemmle with his ability to handle responsibilities, as well as how easily Thalberg understood and explained problems within the company. At the age of 20, Thalberg was given the responsibility of looking after the Los Angeles studio, overseeing multiple film productions at once.

It was not until 1922 that Thalberg met Louis B. Mayer, who was the model for Pat Brady. Mayer was the president of Louis B. Mayer Productions. It was not long before Thalberg and Mayer began working together, as Thalberg left quite an impression on Mayer at their first meeting. Thalberg became vice president in charge of production at Louis B. Mayer Productions. Despite Mayer being a sharp-witted and intelligent businessman, "what he lacked was Thalberg's almost unerring ability to combine quality with commercial success, to bring artistic aspiration in line with the demands of the box office" (Roland, 1994).

In 1924, Metro-Goldwyn-Mayer was established from the amalgamation of three separate studios: the Metro Studio, Sam Goldwyn Productions, and Louis B. Mayer Productions. Mayer was the studio boss within MGM, with Thalberg right underneath him.

THE AMERICAN DREAM

One of the key themes explored in *The Last Tycoon* is the American Dream, which is defined by the Merriam-Webster dictionary as "a happy way of living that is thought of by many Americans as something that can be achieved by anyone in the U.S. especially by working hard and becoming successful".

The novel explores the theme of the American Dream from multiple angles. On the one hand, there is Mr. Schwartz, who is revealed to be an unsuccessful screenwriter. Mr. Schwartz evidently represents the darker side of the American Dream. He tried to make it in the industry, and worked for his screenplays to be accepted and seen, but nonetheless, he did not succeed.

It could be argued that a lack of real effort is the reason for his lack of success, but this is not explored in the novel, so we can only imagine what his life was like pre-*The Last Tycoon*. We cannot say for sure what he did in order to push his way into the industry. In any case, it did not work out for Mr. Schwartz, and thus the ideal of the American Dream, and his failure to reach it, resulted in Mr. Schwartz's suicide.

At the opposite end of this scale, we have Monroe Stahr. In contrast to Mr. Schwartz, Stahr has achieved his goal of becoming a famous Hollywood producer, and has even risen to the top of the film industry thanks to his talents, abilities and drive. As stated previously, Stahr dives into work after the death of his wife, which gives his career a further boost.

Stahr's film studio is where he spends a lot of his time. Chapter 3 of *The Last Tycoon* lays out his typical working day:

> "It was noon already and the conferees were en-
> titled to exactly an hour of Stahr's time. No less,
> for such a conference could only be interrupted
> by a director who was held up in his shooting;

> seldom much more because every eight days the company must release a production as complex and costly as Reinhardt's 'Miracle'." (p. 37)

Nevertheless, while we see that Stahr's hard work has brought him success within the industry, this does not come without consequences. It becomes clear that Stahr's partner, Brady, wants to be rid of him, and to do this, he hires a hitman to kill him. To defend himself, Stahr retaliates with his own hitman. As one critic has put it, "These nefarious plots indicate to the reader that the so-called land of opportunity has become a dangerous place where jealousy is apt to destroy those who try to get ahead" (Locklear, enotes.com).

While the American Dream may have been built up to be seen as something that is easily achievable, there are still obstacles, and despite the hard work, there will still be those who try to tear you down. Stahr and Brady are representations of this idea: one achieves his dreams, but the other's jealousy gets the better of him, and it does not end well for either man.

THE THEME OF DESTRUCTION

Within the novel, there is not a single character who does not go through multiple trials and tribulations. We see characters crumble and fall, and mostly fail to pick themselves back up again. This could be interpreted as a domino effect: when one character falls, the rest are soon to follow.

Firstly, there are Mr. Schwartz and Wylie Whyte. Mr. Schwartz has already failed in his dream of becoming a successful screenwriter. This failure has destroyed him, and beat him down until he sank into a deep depression, eventually leading him to commit suicide. The destruction that is evident throughout the novel has already begun, and it is not long until the other characters meet the same tragic fate as Mr. Schwartz.

Once Cecilia reaches Los Angeles, we meet her father and Stahr. Stahr's life has already deteriorated after the passing of his wife, although he buries his trauma under his workload. The mental strain that Stahr is under has already brought him to breaking point, and by the end of the novel his destruction is complete

Stahr's fight with schizophrenia also plays a role in his downward spiral. Cecilia tells us that he is losing this fight, and thus, no matter what Stahr does, things will end badly for him. The final destruction, for Stahr, comes when he tries to retaliate against Brady's attempt at his life. After hiring a hitman, Stahr begins to second guess himself, despite Brady trying to murder him. Everything, his mind and body, are being destroyed, or set out to be destroyed.

Brady, on the other hand, has no doubts. His mind has already been corrupted by his jealousy for Stahr. Brady does not want Stahr to be more successful than him, and has wanted to be rid of him for a while. In Brady's mind, the only way he can ensure that this happens is to hire someone to kill his partner. It is clear that Brady has already been destroyed mentally, for no sane person would hatch a plan so cruel.

> "Fitzgerald has planned to end the novel with a funeral, and I think of that funeral which he did not live to write as the consummate symbol of decadent individualism today. All is evil, all must be destroyed before the self can reign again pure and alone." (Embler, 1945)

FURTHER REFLECTION

SOME QUESTIONS TO THINK ABOUT...

- In what other ways could the American Dream be seen as corrupting, or significant?
- While Stahr cares about the creative dimension of filmmaking, Brady simply wants to make money; why do you think Brady became jealous, given that the two had different ideals and goals in the industry?
- Discuss further similarities and differences between Stahr and Brady, and their real-life counterparts, Thalberg and Mayer. In what ways did Fitzgerald draw from his own experiences in regards to working with Thalberg? Do you think Fitzgerald, even subconsciously, inserted himself into the story in order to tell it better?
- Discuss the ways in which the story could have differed had Fitzgerald been the one to finish it. Do you believe that the notes included in the novel give a clear idea of Fitzgerald's thoughts on the novel?

- "In an unguarded admission Fitzgerald describes the book as 'an escape into a lavish, romantic past that perhaps will not come again in our time'" (Troy, 1945: 135). Discuss.
- What effect might the ending – in particular, the deaths of Brady and Stahr – have upon the reader? Do you think they are likely to feel sympathy for any of the characters?
- How does this novel reflect, or relate to, real life, with regard to the American Dream, jealousy, ambition, or other themes?
- Why do you think Fitzgerald started the novel with Cecilia meeting Wylie and Mr. Schwartz, who have been unsuccessful in their careers? In what way is this juxtaposed with later parts of the novel?

We want to hear from you!
Leave a comment on your online library
and share your favourite books on social media!

FURTHER READING

REFERENCE EDITION

- Fitzgerald, F. S. (1941) *The Last Tycoon.* United States: Charles Scribner's Sons.

REFERENCE STUDIES

- (No date) Definition of *the American dream. Merriam-Webster.* [Online]. [Accessed 31 January 2019]. Available from: <https://www.merriam-webster.com/dictionary/the%20American%20dream>

- Embler, W. (1945) F. Scott Fitzgerald and the Future. *Chimera.* [Online]. [Accessed 1 Feb 2019]. Available from: <http://fitzgerald.narod.ru/critics-eng/embler-future.html>

- Flamini, R. (1994) *Thalberg: The Last Tycoon and the World of M-G-M.* New York: Crown.

- Locklear, S. ed. (No date) The Last Tycoon Themes. *eNotes Publishing.* [Online]. [Accessed 31 January 2019]. Available from: <https://www.enotes.com/topics/last-tycoon/themes>

- McGrath, C. (2004) Fitzgerald as Screenwriter: No Hollywood Ending. *The New York Times.* [Online]. [Accessed 31 January 2019]. Available from: <https://www.nytimes.com/2004/04/22/us/fitzgerald-as-screenwriter-no-hollywood-ending.html>

- Troy, W. (1963) Scott Fitzgerald—the Authority of Failure. In: A. Walton Litz, ed. *Modern American Fiction*. Oxford: Oxford University Press.

ADAPTATIONS

- *The Last Tycoon.* (1957) [TV episode]. John Frankenheimer. Dir. United States.

- *The Last Tycoon.* (1976) [Film]. Elia Kazan. Dir. United States: Paramount Pictures.

- *The Last Tycoon.* (1998) [Stage play]. Simon Levy. Dir. United States: The Fountain Theatre.

- *The Last Tycoon.* (2013) [Audio adaptation]. Bill Bryden. Dir. Britain: BBC Radio 4.

- *The Love of the Last Tycoon.* (2014) [Musical]. Japan: Takarazuka Revue.

- *The Last Tycoon.* (2016) [TV series]. Billy Ray. Developer. United States: Amazon Video.

MORE FROM BRIGHTSUMMARIES.COM

- Reading guide – *Tender is the Night* by F. Scott Fitzgerald.

- Reading guide – *The Beautiful and the Damned* by F. Scott Fitzgerald.

- Reading guide – *The Great Gatsby* by F. Scott Fitzgerald.

- Reading guide – *This Side of Paradise* by F. Scott Fitzgerald.

www.brightsummaries.com

Ebook EAN: 9782808017862

Paperback EAN: 9782808018586

Legal Deposit: D/2019/12603/60

Cover: © Primento

Digital conception by Primento, the digital partner of
publishers.